TABLE OF CONTENTS

I0504926

1. Landlords for over 20 years. The Schmidt's bought their first rental in 1994. Gary was working at the UPS and Cynthia at the USPS

2. 75 Rental Units in 2000 with mostly single family homes. We felt that they appreciated and was much sought out.

3. 18 years in the Eviction & Small Claims Court Cynthia represented herself and gained knowledge every court appearance.

4. 16 years in Post-Judgment Proceedings (Debt Collection)

5. *96 satisfied judgments, over $300,000 in the Post-Judgment Proceedings. Hundreds of court appearances with has created a mountain of knowledge and confidence.*

6. Authors & Teachers of the Collect Back Rent Training Course & Assignment of Judgments

7. National Speakers-spoke in 37 states at REIA and Landlord groups. Spoke at the OREIA National Summit, Jeffrey Taylor's cruise and conventions to name a few

8. Mentor to over 3,000 Collect Back Rent & Assignment of Judgments Team Members

Tips for Success in the Courtroom

1. Always pick up the *Proof of Service* documents from the process server at least 2 days prior to the court date.

2. Try to arrive at least 10 minutes early before the call at any of the court procedures to mentally prepare.

3. The courtroom is not for <u>cell phones, beverages</u> or <u>talking</u>. If you don't believe me, try it, you'll find out by the Judge, so heed the warning.

4. I never confront the judgment debtor in the hallways and definitely not at the podium. The Judge has been paid by you to be the mediator and will do the confronting for you. Believe me- try it and find out the results

5. NEVER-NEVER argue with the Judge. Whatever the decision, the Judge makes, he/she is always right! He/she will never reverse their decision because the plaintiff is unsatisfied of the decision

6. Always be prepared with the paperwork that is needed to present to the Judge. Only bring needed documents.

7. Observe how the attorney conduct themselves. Remind yourself that you are entering into their world.

8. Make your court date educational. Take notes and try to listen to other cases attentively. I always sit up close in the courtroom so I can hear the attorney's presentations. The Judge is used to dealing with professionals.

9. Word of advice. Always reply to the Judge in the same way "Thank you Judge," whether you agree with their decision or not. When the Judge makes the decision-that is it!

10. Just remember that you may be seeing the same Judge in the Post-Judgment proceedings so we want to make a good impression.

POST-JUDGMENT PROCEDURES

1. **Record the Judgment**: this can prevent the judgment debtor from selling property or receiving certain benefit If you have a judgment you haven't recorded you can do it now. Best practice right out of being awarded the judgment is to have it recorded

2. **Request for a Licensed Process Server**: some states require th judgment creditor to request for a process server instead of the sheriff to serve documents. Having the **Wage Deduction** or **Bank levy** served by the sheriff is suggested. If you are filing a **Discover** I definitely suggest using a licensed process server.

3. **Wage Deduction (job):** Garnishing the judgment debtor's paycheck or salary. If we don't know where they work you can file a Discovery to obtain that information. You can always have the tenant update the rental application at the yearly lease signing.

4. **Bank Levy:** Garnishing the judgment debtor's bank accounts. A accounts are frozen until the court heating. You may not know where the debtor is banking. You will subpoena bank statements that the debtor will have to ring to the Discovery.

5. **Levy on Personal Property:** Sheriff seizes and sells the judgment debtor's *non-exempt* property. Most of the time the debtor will pay the judgment to avoid a sheriff's sale of the non-exempt personal property.

6. **Discovery:** the judgment creditor summons the judgment debtor back to court to conduct a discovery of assets. This is the court if they fail to appear a Bench Warrant is issued. I collected most of my judgments in this proceedings

1. **FAMILY MEMBERS**

2. **ENEMIES**

3. **ACCURINT.COM**

4. **NETDETECTIVE.COM**

5. **MERLINDATA.COM**

6. **INTELLIUS.COM**

7. **GOOGLE**

8. **OBITUARY SITES**

9. **ANCESTORY SITES**

10. **CLASSMATES**

11. **MYSPACE.COM**

12. **FACEBOOK**

13. **TWITTER**

14. **REVERSE DIRECTORY**

15. **YELLOW PAGE**

16. **WHITE PAGES**

17. **YAHOO PEOPLE SEARCH**

18. DOG PILE

19. DEPARTMENT OF MOTOR VEHICLES

20. LOCAL TRAFFIC

21. INSTAGRAM

22. COURTHOUSE WEBSITES

23. PEOPLESMART.COM

24. BANKRUPTCY COURT

25. ZABA SEARCH

26. COUNTY RECORDER OFFICE

27. STATE BUSINESS LICENSE

28. TREASURER'S OFFICE

29. DEATH INDEX

30. MUGSHOTS.COM

31. IF YOU CAN'T FIND THEM USING THESE WEBSITES THEN YOU CAN *SKIP TRACE BY A PROCESS SERVER*

POST-JUDGMENT FLOWCHART

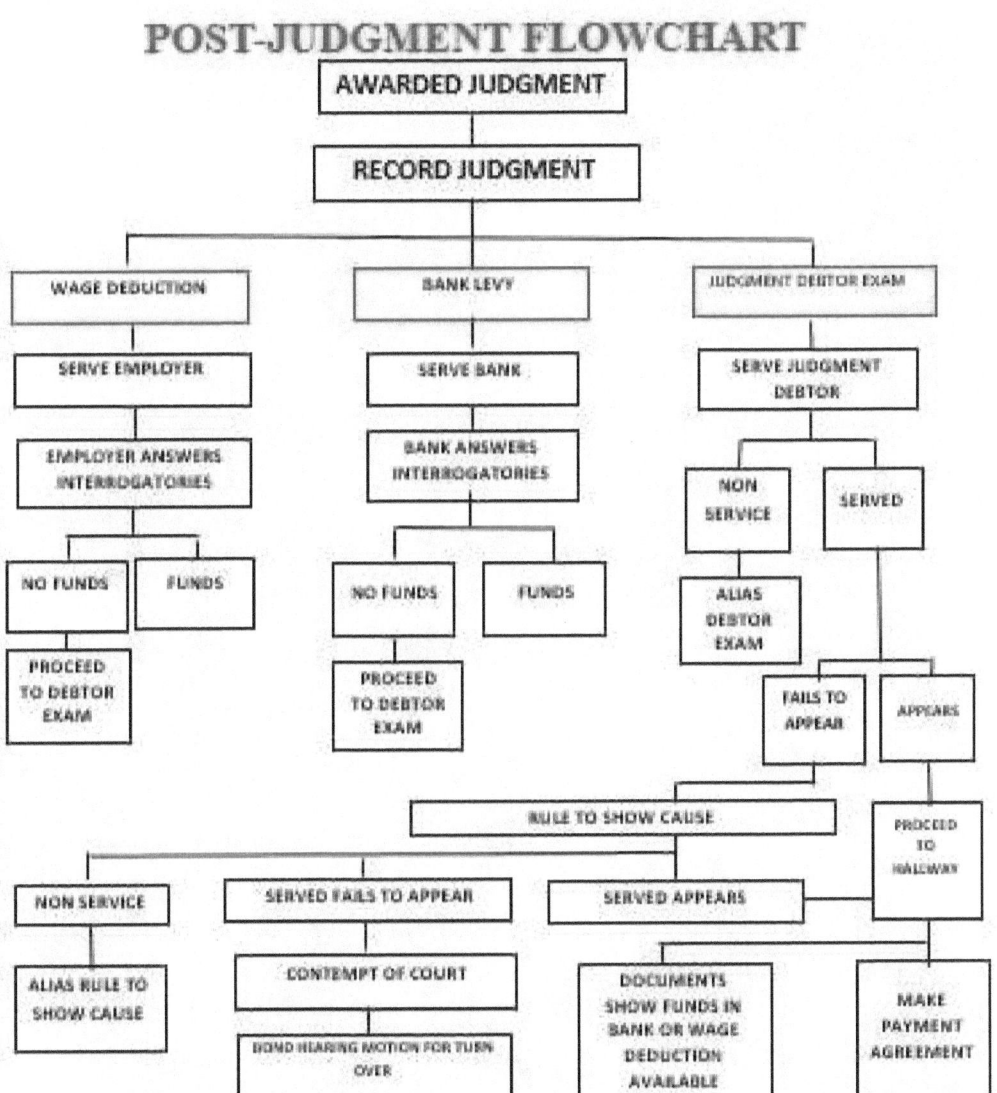

AWARDED JUDGMENT

RECORD JUDGMENT

WAGE DEDUCTION → SERVE EMPLOYER → EMPLOYER ANSWERS INTERROGATORIES → NO FUNDS / FUNDS → PROCEED TO DEBTOR EXAM

BANK LEVY → SERVE BANK → BANK ANSWERS INTERROGATORIES → NO FUNDS / FUNDS → PROCEED TO DEBTOR EXAM

JUDGMENT DEBTOR EXAM → SERVE JUDGMENT DEBTOR → NON SERVICE / SERVED

NON SERVICE → ALIAS DEBTOR EXAM

SERVED → FAILS TO APPEAR / APPEARS

APPEARS → PROCEED TO HALLWAY

RULE TO SHOW CAUSE → NON SERVICE / SERVED FAILS TO APPEAR / SERVED APPEARS

NON SERVICE → ALIAS RULE TO SHOW CAUSE

SERVED FAILS TO APPEAR → CONTEMPT OF COURT → BOND HEARING MOTION FOR TURN OVER

SERVED APPEARS → DOCUMENTS SHOW FUNDS IN BANK OR WAGE DEDUCTION AVAILABLE

PROCEED TO HALLWAY → MAKE PAYMENT AGREEMENT

RECORDING
OF
JUDGMENT

Each of the 50 states has a procedure to record the judgment that is awarded.

The different titles of this procedure can be:

Transcript of Judgment

Judgment Lien Certificate

Abstract of Judgment

Judgment Lien Certificate

Memorandum of Judgment.

After the judgment is awarded, the judgment creditor must obtain an exemplified copy of the judgment. This copy will be filed with the recording of judgment form.

This will attach a lien to any real estate that they may sell in the county and state where they live.

Each state has a time limit to how long the lien is active.

Be sure to research your state's statute concerning the recording of the judgment and if the lien can be revived when it becomes dormant.

Person(s) or Party suing

No. **Same Case Number**

Person(s) or Party being sued

On **Date of Judgment**, 20___, judgment was entered in the court of the plaintiff **Person(s) or Party suing**

Complete address of Person(s) or Party suing

_____

Against **Person(s) or Party being sued**

_____

Last Known Address of Person(s) or Party being sued
_____

Amount of $ **total due**

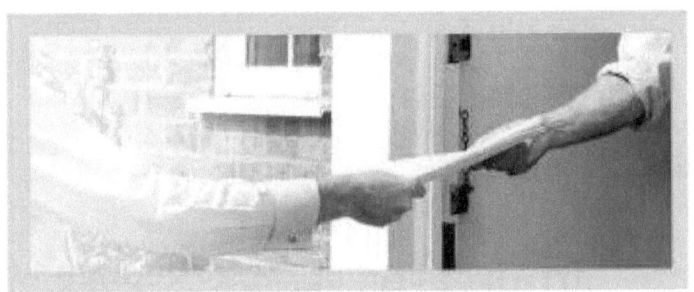

REQUEST FOR LICENSE PROCESS SERVER

Court documents in the Post-Judgment Proceedings have to be served to the Judgment Debtor by the Sheriff or Licensed Process Server. Some of the states allow anyone over 18 years old and not involved with the case to serve the documents.

When you go to court, the *abode* which is a document filled out by the server must be perfect. That is why I strongly recommend using one of the professionals to serve the documents.

The Licensed Process Server is the best because I feel they go the distance to get the documents served. We use a server with the name "Man on a Mission" and he gets those documents served at weddings, funerals, health clubs and local watering holes Get yourself a good process server.

When filing the Post-Judgment documents, the Clerk will ask if the documents are being served by the Sheriff or a Licensed Process Server. Some states require the Judgment Creditor to file the *Request for Appointment of Process Server* when choosing this option.

Person(s) or Party suing

Case No. **Same case number**

Person(s) or Party being sued

REQUEST FOR PROCESS SERVER

Person(s) or Party suing pursuant to **state law** and at their own risk requests the appointment of

Complete name of server

Address of server

(Natural person of lawful age who is not a part of this action) to serve the Affidavit and Summons in this case. This appointment as special server does not include the authorization to carry a concealed weapon in the performance of this duty.

Appointed as requested:

By: **Clerk**

Date: **Clerk**

Requested: **Signature of Person(s) or Party suing**

WAGE
GARNISHMENT

After the judgment is awarded, the Judgment Creditor can file documents with the Court Clerk to issue a Wage Deduction/Garnishment.

The Judgment Creditor will file the *Wage Deduction Notice, Summons, Affidavit and Interrogatories* documents. In the *Affidavit,* the Judgment Creditor states to their belief that the debtor's employer owes the creditor wages. It also states that Judgment Creditor mailed a copy of the *Wage Deduction Notice* to the debtor at the debtor's last known address.

The *Wage Deduction Notice, Summons, Affidavit and Interrogatories* must be served to the employer. Again, I suggest using a professional to serve the documents. When the employer is served the documents, they are notified how long they have to file the *Interrogatories* and the date the case will be heard in court.

At the court hearing, the Judge will be presented the *Proof of Service* and the *Interrogatories* filled out by the employer. At that time the Judgment Creditor will present the *Wage Deduction Order* to the Judge to sign.

Person(s) or Party suing

RETURN DATE: **Clerk**____

Person or Party being sued

Amount of judgment: **Amount of judgment**

Balance Due: **Judgment, court costs, interest**

Name of Employer: **Complete name of employer**_____

WAGE DEDUCTION NOTICE

The court shall be asked to issue a wage deduction summons against employer named above for wage dues or about to become due to the judgment debtor. The wage deduction summons may be issued on the basis of judgment against the judgment debtor in favor of the judgment creditor in the amount stated above.

The amount of wages that may be deducted is limited by federal and state laws.

1) The amount of wages that may be deducted is limited to the lesser of (1) 15% of gross weekly wages or (ii) the amount by which disposable earnings for a week exceed the total of 45 times the federal minimum hourly wage.

2) Under federal law, the amount of wages that may be deducted limited to the lesser of (ii) 25% of disposable wages for a week or (ii) the amount of disposable earnings for a week exceed 30 times the federal minimum hourly wage.

) Pension and retirement benefits and refunds may be claimed exempt from wage deduction under **Name of state** law.

Person(s) or Party suing

       VS

Person or Party being sued
complete address of employer
and   **Name of Employer**

WAGE DEDUCTION SUMMONS

To the Employer:

YOU ARE SUMMONED and required to file answers to the judgment creditor's interrogatories, in the Office of the Clerk of Court _____**Clerk**_____ on or before _____**Clerk**_ _____, 20__

However, if this summons is served on you less than 3 days before that date, you must file answers to the interrogatories on or before a new return date, to be set by the court, not less than 21 days after you were served the summons.

This proceeding applies to non-exempt wages due at the time you were served with this summons and to wages which become due thereafter until the balance due on the judgment is paid.

IF YOU FAIL TO ANSWER, A CONDITIONAL JUDGMENT BY DEFAULT MAY BE TAKEN AGAINST YOU FOR THE AMOUNT OF THE JUDGMENT UNPAID.

FEDERAL AGENCY EMPLOYEES: Effective upon service of this summons and pursuant to 5 USC 552 (a) you are to commence to pay deducted wages to the attorney for the judgment creditor in accordance with **state law.**

Person(s) or Party suing

Person or Party being sued

Return Date: **Clerk**

Name of Employer

AFFIDAVIT FOR SUMMONS

_____ **Person(s) or Party suing** _____ on oath states:

1. I believe the employer **Name of Employer** _____ is indebted to the judgment debtor **Person or Party being sued** _____for wages due or to become due. Employer's address is **Address of Employer**

2. The last known address of the judgment debtor is **Address of Person or Party being sued** _____

_____

request that a summons issue directed to the employer and I certify that a copy of the Wage Deduction Notice was mailed to the judgment debtor, by first class mail. At his/her address prior to filing of this wage deduction proceeding.

Name **Person(s) or Party suing** _____

AFFIANT: **Signature of Person(s) or Party suing** _____

CERTIFCATE OF ATTORNEY OR JUDGMENT CREDITOR

1. Judgment in the above case was entered **Date of Judgment**

2. The amount of Judgment was $**Amount of Judgment**

3. Allowable costs
a. Initial filing $ **Forcible Detainer** ___
b. Original and alias summons $ **Court Costs** _____
c. Filing and summons costs of
prior supplementary proceeding $_____

4. Filing and summons costs-wage $ **Costs for wage** _____

5. Statutory interest due on judgment $ **Check State Statute** __
                              Total $ **Judgment, Court Costs**
                                            & Interest
DEDUCT: amount paid by judgment $ **monies received** debtor
prior to this proceedings

BALANCE DUE JUDGMENT CREDITOR $ **Total minus any monies**

Signature of Person(s) or Party suing _____

FILLED OUT BY EMPLOYER

Return Date_____

Case Number:_____

INTERROGATORIES TO WAGE DEDUCTION PROCEEDINGS

Employer/Agent_____, certifies under penalty of perjury that the following Answer is true and correct to the best of her/his knowledge and belief concerning the property of the judgment debtor.

Debtor Name: _____

Soc. Sec. No. _____

Do you pay monies to the judgment debtor listed above? Yes No

State whether any funds paid to the debtor are for disability, retirement or are any other way exempt or subject to other.

One Pay Period equals ___ day(s)_____ week(s)_____ month(s)

Person(s) or Party suing

Person or Party being sued
and
Name of Employer

HIS CAUSE coming on to be heard upon the return of a Wage Deduction Summons served upon the employer and the answer filed by the employer, a Wage Deduction Notice having been served upon the employee and the Court fully advised.

IT IS HEREBY ORDERED:

1. That a lien is hereby imposed upon the non-exempt wages of **Person or Party being sued** as of the date of the service of the Wage Deduction Summons in the amount of $**Total due** which includes court costs and interest to date and credit for payments to date.

2. That **Employer** is ordered to deduct from the wages of the judgment debtor an amount not to exceed the lesser of (i) 15% of the defendant's gross wages.
3. That a Wage Deduction judgment is hereby entered against Employer, **Employer** in the periodic sum ordered above for each pay period in favor of Defendant, **Person or Party being sued** for the use of the Plaintiff, **Person or Party suing** .

Judge

Writ of Execution–Bank Levy

GARNISHING THE BANKING INSTITUTION

After the judgment is awarded, one of the procedures to collect is the Non-Wage Deduction referred to as a Bank Levy. The Judgment Creditor is attaching a garnishment to the Judgment Debtor's savings, checking and money market accounts.

The Judgment Creditor will file the *Non-Wage Deduction Notice, Affidavit and Respondent's Answer* documents with the Clerk.

The Clerk will issue a time for the Bank to file the *Respondent's Answer* and a court date.

All parties with an interest in the case must be sent a copy of the *Non-Wage Deduction Notice.* This gives the Judgment Debtor an opportunity to pay the judgment prior to use of garnishment remedy by the Judgment Creditor

Non-Wage Deduction Notice, Affidavit and Respondent's Answer documents must be served to the Banking Institution notifying them of the time allotted to file the *Respondent's Answer* and court date. The Banking Institution will send a copy of the *Respondent's Answer* to the Judgment Creditor prior to the court hearing.

At the court heating, the Judge will be presented the *Proof of Service* and the *Respondent's Answer.* The Judge will examine the *Respondent's Answer* to clarify the funds to be attached in the Judgment Debtor's bank accounts.

When the Judge renders a decision, the Judgment Creditor will present the *Order*. This *Order* will be filled out correctly stating the Names, Banking Institutions and how much of the funds can be attached.

When the Judgment Debtor has multiple Banking Institution accounts, the Judgment Creditor will file a Bank Levy on each one of them.

At the hearing, the Judgment Creditor would need:

Proof of Service

Respondent's Answer

Order for each of the Banks.

Person(s) or Party suing _

Person(s) or Party being sued

Amount of Judgment $ **Judgment Amt.**
Court Date and Time: **Clerk**
Name of person receiving notice: **Person(s) or Party being sued**

NON-WAGE DEDUCTION NOTICE

NOTICE: The court has issued a non-wage deduction notice against the person named above. The notice is to notify the judgment debtor of a non-wage deduction proceeding is be taken against the person named above. If the judgment debtor has exemptions under state law to be declared, the judgment debtor must file in writing at **Name & address of courthouse** before the court date and time listed above.

The Clerk will provide a hearing date and the necessary forms that must be prepared by the judgment debtor or the attorney for the judgment debtor and send to the judgment creditor regarding the time and location of the hearing. This action may be sent by regular first class mail

Person(s) or Party suing

Person(s) or Party being sued

Name of Banking Institution

AFFIDAVIT OF NON-WAGE DEDUCTION

O: **Name and complete address of Banking Institution**

OU ARE REQUIRED to appear and/or file your answer to the ffidavit on the form on the next page hereof (or appropriate nswer) on **Clerk** ,20___ prior to ___AM/PM in Courtroom ____ of the Court of **Name and address of Courthouse** .

judgment against **Person(s) or Party being sued** as entered on **date of Judgment** and $ **Total due** emains unsatisfied.

OU ARE PROHIBITED from making any transfer or other sposition of, or interfering with any property exempt from xecution or garnishment belonging to the judgment debtor or to hich the judgment debtor may be entitled or which may be cquired by or become due to the judgment debtor until further rder of court or termination of the proceedings. You are not equired to withhold of any money beyond double the amount of alance due.

JDGMENT AMOUNT: **Judgment Amt.**

ALANCE DUE: **Judgment, Court Costs**

ATE OF JUDGMENT: **Date Judgment as awarded**

/ITNESS: **Clerk**

FILLED OUT BY BANKING INSTITUTION

CASE NO. _____

HEARING DATE: _____

THIRD PARTY RESPONDENT TO AFFIDAVIT

_____ _____ certifies under penalty of perjury that with regard to the property of the judgment debtor, the Affidavit Respondent files the following answer to this Non-Wage Deduction and is in possession of the following property of the judgment debtor.

Circle one or more of the following and indicate the amount held:

A) Savings Account (Amount withheld): $_____

B) Checking and or Now Account (Amount withheld):$_____

C) Certificate of Deposit (Amount held $_____

D) Money Market Account (Amount held) $_____

E) Trust Account (Amount held) $_____

F) Safety Deposit Box $_____

SUB-TOTAL $_____

Less right of offset for other loan TOTAL $_____

According to the business records kept by the Affidavit Respondent, we show the above information is correct.

Person(s) or Party suing

Case No. **Same case number**

Person(s) or Party being sued

ORDER

Plaintiff appears/by attorney **Pro-se**

_Defendant appears/by attorney_____

_Cause set for trial on _____ at _____AM/PM

THIS IS THE ONLY NOTICE YOU WILL RECEIVE OF THE TRIAL DATE. YOU MUST FILE A WRITTEN APPEARANCE AND (IF APPLICABLE) PAY A FEE OR YOU MAY BE FOUND IN DEFAULT.

_ Motion of Plaintiff/Defendant for _____ is granted/denied

_ Judgment entered for Plaintiff against Defendant(s) _____ in the sum of $_____ plus court costs

_ Defendant _____having failed to appear on _____, the Court issues this Rule To Show Cause, hearing on _____ at _____AM/PM

SHOULD YOU FAIL TO APPEAR IN RESPONSE TO THE RULE ISSUED YOU MAY BE FOUND IN CONTEMP FOR THE FAILURE TO APPEAR, AND A BENCH WARRANT MAY ISSUE FOR YOUR ARREST.

Ordered: **Upon motion of the (Name of Person(s) or Party suing), funds in the amount of ($) held by (Name of Banking Institution) will be turned over to (Name of Person(s) or Party suing).** _____

_____ **Judge** _____

WRIT OF EXECUTION- PERSONAL PROPERTY

SEIZING NON-EXEMPT PERSONAL PROPERTY

Every State has a law concerning exempt property of the Judgment Debtor that is sheltered from the Levy on Personal Property proceedings. Be sure to study your State's Statute concerning the Levy on Personal Property.

When the Judgment Creditor discovers the Judgment Debtor has non-exempt property in their possession, the Judgment Creditor will file a Levy on Personal Property.

The *Instructions for Levy* and *Execution* documents must be filed with the Clerk. After the Clerk issues the Levy, the Judgment Creditor will take the *Instructions for Levy* and *Execution* documents to the Sheriff's office. This directs the Sheriff to levy the property described.

When the Sheriff seizes the non-exempt property to sell, the Judgment Debtor is notified of the date of the sale.

The Judgment Debtor can redeem the property and the funds will be forwarded to the Judgment Creditor credited towards the judgment.

Person(s) or Party suing

Address

Case No. **Same case number**

Person(s) or Party being sued

Complete address

Name of Person(s) holding title
of said property

INSTRUCTIONS FOR LEVY

1. Plaintiff(s) **Person(s) or Party suing** was awarded a Final Judgment in this case on **Date of judgment**, in the amount of $ **Total amount.**

The amount of the Judgment unsatisfied is $ **Balance due.**

2. Plaintiff(s) believes that Defendant(s) owns the following property described as:

2010 Harley Davidson motorcycle (Fat Boy) number 001-000-543

_____

_____

3. That the above-described property is located at: **Address where the property is located**

Person(s) or Party suing\
Address of Person(s) suing

Case No. **Same case number**

Person(s) or Party being sued

Address of Person(s) being sued

EXECUTION

THE STATE OF **Name of State** :\
To Each Sheriff of the State:

YOU ARE HEREBY COMMANDED to levy on the goods and chattels, lands, and tenements of **Person(s) or Party being sued** in the sum of $ **Total amount** with legal interest thereon from **date of judgment** 20___, until paid and that you have this writ before the court when satisfied.

WITNESS my hand and the seal of the court: **Clerk**_____, 20___.

(SEAL)   By: __**Clerk**_____

DISCOVERY

This procedure is the "KEY" to collecting on unpaid judgments. I collected 62 of my 96 satisfied judgments in this proceeding. I stumbled into this Court in 1998 and was the only Judgment Creditor that represented themselves in there for 8 years. Every court date I would look around for other landlords which never came and it was full of **lawyers.**

Every State has this procedure in which the Judgment Creditor summons the Judgment Debtor to court.

This procedure can be called:

Citation to Discover Assets

Motion In Aid of Execution

Subpoena Order to appear and Produce Documents

Debtor's Examination

This is why I labeled this procedure: ***Discovery*** because the Judgment Creditor summons the Judgment Debtor to court to conduct a ***Discovery.***

The Judgment Creditor will file a *Discovery Notice, Discovery and Rider to Discovery* with the Clerk. The Clerk will issue a court date where the Creditor and Debtor must appear. The *Discovery Notice, Discovery and Rider to Discover* must be served to the Debtor by the Sheriff or Process Server.

At the court hearing, the Judgment Creditor will give the *Proof of Service* to the Judge. When the Judgment Debtor appears, the Judge will instruct the Judgment Creditor and Judgment Debtor to proceed out into the hallway.

This is the Judgment Creditor's opportunity to conduct a **_Discovery_** with the Judgment Debtor to the documents that was subpoenaed.

 The Judgment Creditor will examine:

Judgment Debtor's Tax Returns (possible refund)

Pay-Roll Stubs (Wage Deduction)

Bank Statements (Bank Levy)

Registration to all Vehicles (Levy on Personal Property).

When the Judgment Creditor is conducting the **_Discovery_** on the Judgment Debtor, there is a possibility of making a monthly payment agreement. When explained to the Judgment Debtor that this is not going to go away and interest is accruing sometimes this is the answer.

When a payment is agreed on, the Judgment Creditor will fill out the *Order* and present to the Judge to sign.

If the Judgment Debtor fails to answer the Judgment Creditors questions or failed to bring demanded documents, the Judgment will proceed back into the courtroom.

When called back up to the podium, the Judgment Creditor will explain the Judgment Debtor is not cooperating. At that time, the Judge will take over.

Person(s) or Party suing _____

Case No. **Same case number**

Person(s) or Party being sued ____

DISCOVERY

Person(s) or Party being sued ___

Complete address _____

YOU ARE HEREBY COMMANDED to appear before the Judge presiding in Room __ of the **Name of courthouse**, **Address of courthouse, Name of City, Name of State** on _____ **Clerk** ____, 20___, at _____ to be examined under oath to discover assets or income not exempt from enforcement of the judgment.
YOU ARE COMMANDED to produce at the examination: All books, papers in your possession or control which may contain information concerning the property or income of, or indebtedness due judgment debtor and: **SEE ATTACHED RIDER TO DISCOVERY** _____

YOU ARE PROHIBITED from allowing transfer any property not exempt from execution or garnishment belonging to the judgment debtor.

YOUR FAILURE TO APPEAR TO THIS HEARING CAN RESULT IN YOUR ARREST WHICH MAY RESULT IN IMPRISONMENT

JUDGMENT AMOUNT: **Amt. of Judgment** ___
BALANCE DUE **Judgment, court costs & interest**

ATTACHED RIDER TO DISCOVERY

Please bring the following document to your Discovery Court appearance:

1. 2017. 2018, 2019 Federal and State income tax returns

2. One (1) year on bank statements (checking and savings

3. One (1) year of 401k statements.

4. Registration of all vehicles (autos, boats and campers) under your name.

5. Two (2) recent pay-roll stubs.

6. 2019 W-2 form

Person(s) or Party suing

Case No. **Same case number**

Person(s) or Party being sued

ORDER

x Plaintiff appears/by attorney **Pro-se**

x Defendant appears/by attorney **Pro-se**

__ Cause set for trial on _____ at _____ AM/PM

THIS IS THE ONLY NOTICE YOU WILL RECEIVE OF THE TRIAL DATE. YOU MUST FILE A WRITTEN APPEARANCE AND (IF APPLICABLE) PAY A FEE OR YOU MAY BE FOUND IN DEFAULT.

__ Motion of Plaintiff/Defendant for _____ is granted/denied

__ Judgment entered for Plaintiff against Defendant(s) _____ in the sum of $_____ plus court costs

__ Defendant _____ having failed to appear on _____, the Court issues this Rule To Show Cause, hearing on _____ at _____ AM/PM

SHOULD YOU FAIL TO APPEAR IN RESPONSE TO THE RULE ISSUED YOU MAY BE FOUND IN CONTEMP FOR THE FAILURE TO APPEAR, AND A BENCH WARRANT MAY ISSUE FOR YOUR ARREST.

Ordered: **Agreed monthly payment between (Name of Person suing) and (Name of Person(s) or Party being sued) of $ and starting on the first of (Month) and on the first of every month after until judgment is satisfied.**

RULE TO SHOW CAUSE

RULE TO SHOW CAUSE-FAILURE TO APPEAR

At the **_Discovery_** court hearing, the Judgment Creditor will present the Judge the *Proof of Service* of the *Discovery and Rider to* Discovery.

When the Judgment Debtor appears, the Judgment Creditor and Debtor will proceed into the courtroom hallway to conduct the **_Discovery._**

If the Judgment Debtor **fails to appear,** the Judgment Creditor will motion for a *Rule to Show Cause to Issue* court date. This is a second notice to come to court or the Judge will issue Bench Warrant for the Debtor. The Rule to Show Cause document must be personally served to the Debtor. Debtor is the only one that can accept service.

By issuing another court date, the Judge gives the Judgment Debtor a second chance to appear to the court proceedings.

The Judgment Creditor will present the Judge with the *Rule to Show Cause* and the *Order* to sign.

These documents must be served personally to the Judgment Debtor notifying them of the time and place of the Rule to Show Cause to Issue court hearing.

Person(s) or Party suing

 Case No. **Same case number**

Person or Party being sued

Person(s) or Party being sued
complete address

RULE TO SHOW CAUSE TO ISSUE

YOU ARE HEREBY ORDERED to appear on the date _____ at ___
_____ am/pm. In Courtroom __ of the **X Name and address of**
Courthouse , Name of City, Name of State
_____

Before the Presiding Judge and **SHOW CAUSE WHY YOU SHOULD
NOT BE HELD IN CONTEMPT OF COURT** for your failure to abide
with Previous Orders of the Court.

**IF YOU FAIL TO APPEAR ON THE ABOVE DATE, THE COURT WILL
ISSUE A BENCH WARRANT FOR YOUR ARREST.**

Date: **Judge**

Enter: **Judge**

Person(s) or Party suing

Case No. **Same case number**

Person(s) or Party being sued

ORDER

x Plaintiff appears/by attorney **Pro-se**

_Defendant appears/by attorney **FTA**

_Cause set for trial on _____ at _____AM/PM

THIS IS THE ONLY NOTICE YOU WILL RECEIVE OF THE TRIAL DATE. YOU MUST FILE A WRITTEN APPEARANCE AND (IF APPLICABLE) PAY A FEE OR YOU MAY BE FOUND IN DEFAULT.

_ Motion of Plaintiff/Defendant for _____ is granted/denied

_ Judgment entered for Plaintiff against Defendant(s) _____

_ in the sum of $_____ plus court costs

Defendant **Person or Party being sued** having failed to appear in **Date of hearing**, the Court issues this Rule To Show Cause, hearing on **Judge awards** at _____AM/PM

SHOULD YOU FAIL TO APPEAR IN RESPONSE TO THE RULE ISSUED YOU MAY BE FOUND IN CONTEMP FOR THE FAILURE TO APPEAR, AND A BENCH WARRANT MAY ISSUE FOR YOUR ARREST.

Ordered: _____

Date: __**Judge**_____

Signature of Judge_____

BENCH WARRANT

At the Rule to Show Cause to Issue hearing, the Judgment Creditor will present with the *Proof of Service* of the *Rule to Show Cause to Issue* to the Judge, When the Judgment Debtor appears, the Creditor and Debtor will proceed to the courtroom hallway for the **_Discovery._**

If the Judgment Debtor **fails to appear,** the Judgment Creditor will motion for the Judge to issue a **Bench Warrant**.

The Judge will award a bond dollar amount to be attached. At the time the Judgment Creditor will present the *Warrant for Arrest* and the *Order* to the Judge to sign.

When the Judgment Debtor is arrested and posts the dollar amount awarded by the Judge, the funds will be applied to the judgment amount.

The Judgment Debtor is notified by the Court that a **Bench Warrant** was issued against them and they can come to Court to get it resolved.

THE PEOPLE OF THE STATE OF **Name of State**

Case No. **Same case number** __

Person or Party being

WARRANT OF ARREST

TO ALL PEACE OFFICERS OF THE STATE OF **Name of State**

YOU ARE COMMANDED TO ARREST **Person of Party being sued complete address of Person or Party being sued** Gender **M/F** DOB **Date of birth**

Signature of Person(s) or Party suing

AND BRING SAID PERSON WITHOUT UNNECESSARY DELAY BEFORE THE HONORABLE **Judge Presiding** OF THE **Name of Courthouse** USUALLY OCCUPIED BY HIM OR HE/SHE IS ABSENT OR UNABLE TO ACT, BEFORE THE NEAREST OR MOST ACCESSIBLE COURT IN SAID COUNTY, TO ANSWER A CHARGE AGAINST PERSON FOR THE OFFENSE OF:

(CHECK ONE) ___ FAILURE TO APPEAR ___CONTEMPT OF COURT
_____

AND HOLD SAID PERSON TO BAIL OF $ **Amount Judge Awarded**

GEOGRAPHICAL LIMIT ON THE EXECUTION OF THIS WARRANT:
_____ **COUNTY WARRANT WAS ISSUED** _____

_____ **JUDGE** _____

Person(s) or Party suing _____

Case No. **Same case number**

Person(s) or Party being sued ____

ORDER

x Plaintiff appears/by attorney **Pro-se**

__Defendant appears/by attorney **FTA**

__Cause set for trial on _____ at _____AM/PM

HIS IS THE ONLY NOTICE YOU WILL RECEIVE OF THE TRIAL DATE. OU MUST FILE A WRITTEN APPEARANCE AND (IF APPLICABLE) AY A FEE OR YOU MAY BE FOUND IN DEFAULT.

__ Motion of Plaintiff/Defendant for _____ is ranted/denied

__ Judgment entered for Plaintiff against Defendant(s) _____ in 1e sum of $_____ plus court costs

__ Defendant _____having failed to opear on _____, the Court issues this Rule To Show ause, hearing on _____ at _____AM/PM

__ Defendant **Name of Person or Party being sued** having fails to low in response to "Rule To Show Cause To Issue", bench arrant to issue for **Person being sued** bond **Judge awards** sh.

rdered: _____

ate: __**Judge**____

JUDGMENT
SATISFIED

Judgment Debtor Satisfies Judgment

When the Judgment Debtor satisfies the judgment, court costs and interest, the Judgment Creditor must file a *Release of Satisfaction of Judgment* form.

.Make sure that the judgment is completely paid before filing.

The Clerk will index the *Release of Satisfaction of Judgment* in the court records.

The Judgment Creditor will send a copy of the *Release of Satisfaction of Judgment* document to the Judgment Debtor

It is the responsibility of the Judgment Debtor to record in the County Recorder's office.

Person(s) or Party suing

No. **Same Case Number**

Person(s) or Party being sued

RELEASE SATISFACTION OF JUDGMENT

Person(s) or Party suing

_____

Having received full satisfaction and payment, release the judgment

Entered on **Date of Judgment** 20___ against **Person(s) or Party**

Being sued for $ **Judgment Amount** and costs.

Dated: **Date of filing**

Approved:

Signature of Person(s) suing